Dad, Tell Me Your Story

A Father's Guided Journal and Memory Keepsake Book

This journal belongs to :

from your child :

Tell it All Books

ISBN: 978-1-961443-15-0

Published by Harbour House Publishing Press

Printed in the United States of America
Cover design by Victor Oj
Editor and Illustrator: Elsie Bloomfield

Dedicated to my Sons
Valen, vishal & Videl

HOUSE PUBLISHING LTD

Tell it All Books

table of content

Tell it All Books

introduction

This journal is designed specifically for fathers of all kinds, whether biological or non-biological, to capture and preserve the significant moments that have shaped your life.

Dad, Tell Me Your Story™

----Dad ----

It's time to write the story of your life with this guided journal.

It's designed to be filled out with an erasable pen or pencil, whichever you prefer.

As you work through the prompts in this journal, you will have the opportunity to record all the important phases of your life, from childhood to elderhood.

You will be able to reflect on your relationships, your achievements, and the challenges you faced. And as you do so, you will be creating a legacy for your grandchildren and future generations to treasure.

In addition to the prompts provided, this journal also includes special pages where you can document your bucket lists, your travels, your hobbies and interests, birthdays, special milestones, memories, and more.

We hope this journal will be a source of joy and fulfillment as you document your life story. Let's get writing!

Tell it All Books

getting the most out of this journal

welcome to this guided journal! It's important to remember that there are no strict rules or guidelines for using this book. The format is flexible, allowing you to tackle the questions in any order you choose. Whether you prefer to skip around or work through them in order, the choice is yours.

As you respond to each question, there is no right or wrong way to answer. You may choose to skip certain questions or replace them with additional ones available on our website. It's important to write freely and record whatever comes to mind and heart without overthinking or holding back. The best answers are the ones that come straight from the heart, without worrying about perfection or formality.

Take your time with answering the questions. As there are many of them, you may want to complete the book over multiple sessions, dedicating some time each day over a period of weeks or months. You can also enlist the help of a family member to ask you the questions out loud and record your answers on video or audio.

HINT:
- When telling your story, use specific details such as first and last names, exact dates, locations, and brand names.
- Describing things like "mist-green 1945 Cadillac" instead of "...Dad's Car" and "... red roses" instead of "flowers" helps make your story more vivid.
- Also, be precise, such as "...Schrafft's on seventh Street, downtown," instead of "...at Schrafft's." This approach will bring your story to life and make it more engaging.

If you need more space to answer a question, you can utilize the extra notes pages at the end of each section or include memorable photos. Remember to go easy on yourself and enjoy the process of reflecting on your life experiences.

Tell it All Books

...my details, time capsule and family tree.

chapter 1:
the family tree

In this first chapter of our guided journal session, I'd like for us to explore our family tree together. I want to know the stories and experiences that shaped our lineage, and understand the deep connections that bind us all. By diving into our family history, I believe we can strengthen our bond and appreciate the unique tapestry that makes us who we are.

Our family tree is more than just a collection of names and dates; it's a living legacy, filled with the love, joy, heartache, and struggles of the generations before us. I know that you hold many of these stories close to your heart, and I hope that by sharing them with me, you'll feel a sense of pride and fulfillment.

This exercise is important to me because it allows me to connect with my roots and discover a part of myself I may have never known.

By understanding where we come from, we can better understand ourselves and our place in the world. For you, Dad, I hope that this exercise gives you the opportunity to reflect on your own journey and relive memories that may have faded with time.

To make this process as meaningful as possible, I encourage you to be open, honest, and candid in your responses. Don't be afraid to share the emotions that certain memories evoke, whether they are joyous or painful. This is a safe space for you to express yourself and share your story.

As we embark on this journey, I hope we can uncover the emotions, the struggles, and the triumphs that have shaped our family. Let's embrace our past and celebrate the rich tapestry of lives that have come together to create our unique story. Thank you, Dad, for taking the time to share this part of yourself with me.

MY DETAILS

Full Name
_____

Place of Birth
_____

Eye Color
_____

Hair Color
_____

Height
_____

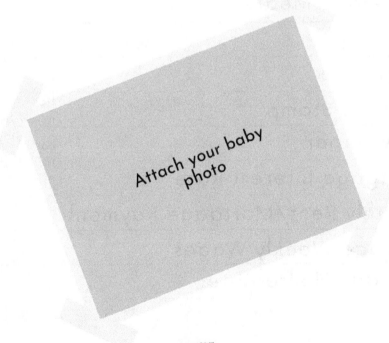

Attach your baby photo

Tell it All Books

time capsule

The Price of...

Gallon of Milk	
Gallon of Gasoline	
Movie Ticket	
Landline Telephone	
Pair of Jeans	
Vinyl Music Album	
Loaf of Bread	
Movie Rental (VHS)	
Fast-Food Meal	
New Car	
Magazine	
Postage Stamp	
Newspaper	
Mortgage Interest Rate	
Monthly Rent/Mortgage Payment	
Average Weekly Wages	
Average House Rate	

FAMILY TREE

Your Great
Grandmother

Your Great
Grandfather

Your Great
Grandmother

Your Great
Grandfather

Your
Grandmother

Your
Grandfather

Your Father

Your Brothers

You

FAMILY TREE

Your Great
Grandmother

Your Great
Grandfather

Your Great
Grandmother

Your Great
Grandfather

Your
Grandmother

Your
Grandfather

Your Mother

Your Sisters

YOUR FAVOURITE.......

Color

Number

Flower

Animal

Films

Actors

Songs

Musicians

Books

Authors

Seasons

Country

TV Series

Weather

getting to know you more...

Food:

Drink:

Color:

Hobby:

Song:

Show:

Games:

App:

City:

Country:

...growing up

Tell it All Books

Chapter 2:
growing up

As we continue our guided journal journey, I'd like to turn our focus to your childhood and the experiences that shaped you into the person you are today. Your "Growing Up" years were a time of discovery, learning, and growth, and I'm eager to understand the joys and challenges you faced during this period.

Our experiences growing up play a significant role in molding our character, values, and beliefs. By understanding your upbringing, I hope to gain insight into the man you've become, and better appreciate the decisions and paths you've taken in life. Your story is an integral part of my own, and I believe that by learning about your past, we can forge a deeper connection and strengthen our bond.

As you reminisce about your childhood and teenage years, I encourage you to reflect on both the happy and difficult moments.

Sharing these memories will not only help me understand the context of your life but also provide valuable life lessons and insights that I can cherish and learn from.

By exploring your "Growing Up" years, we can celebrate the journey that has led you to where you are today. Your experiences, both good and bad, have shaped you, and I'm grateful for the opportunity to understand and appreciate your story.

I'm looking forward to learning more about the younger version of you, and the world that surrounded you as you grew up.

this or that

extravert	introvert
books	movies
art	sport
burger	pizza
juice	soda
dark	light
academia	academia
dogs	cats

Growing Up

When and where were you born? ....

....

....

....

....

....

....

....

....

Where did you grow up? ....

....

....

....

....

....

....

....

....

Growing Up

What was it like? ....

....

....

....

....

....

....

How would you describe yourself as a child? Were you happy? ....

....

....

....

....

....

....

....

....

....

....

....

Growing Up

What is one of your best memories of childhood? Worst? ....

....

....

....

....

....

....

....

....

....

Did you have a nickname? How'd you get it? ....

....

....

....

....

....

....

....

Growing Up

Do you have any favorite stories from your childhood? ....

....

....

....

....

....

....

....

....

....

When you were a child, what did you want to be when you grew up?........................

....

....

....

....

....

....

....

....

Other Things

Other Things

....

....

....

....

....

....

....

....

....

....

....

....

....

....

....

....

....

....

....

...family heirtage

Tell it All Books

this or that

Coffee	Tea
Chesee Cake	Cupcake
Mounth	Beach
Pizza	Burger
Paris	Hawai
Flat Shoes	Casual Shoes
Hot	Ice
Cooking	Reading
Music	Karaoke

Tell it All Books

Chapter 3:
Family Heritage

As your son/daughter, I've always been curious about our family's heritage and the stories that have shaped us into who we are today. In this guided journal session, I'd like to embark on a journey with you to uncover our family's roots, and in the process, deepen our connection with each other. This chapter, "Family Heritage," aims to provide a strong foundation for the rest of our journey.

I believe that by exploring our family's heritage, we can gain a better understanding of our identity and values. Knowing where we come from can help us appreciate the struggles and sacrifices our ancestors made to provide us with the opportunities we have today. It can also help us understand the cultural traditions and customs that have been passed down through generations.

This chapter will give us the opportunity to reflect on our family's history, and to think about what elements of our heritage we want to preserve and pass on to future generations. It will also allow us to explore any difficult or painful experiences that may have impacted our family, and to understand how those experiences have shaped us.

I hope that by sharing your memories and stories with me, we can create a deeper emotional connection and build a stronger bond. Your words and experiences are a precious gift, and I am grateful for the opportunity to learn more about you and our family.

So, let us begin this journey together and discover the richness and diversity of our family's heritage.

Family

Who were your parents? ....
....
....
....
....
....
....
....
....
....
....

What were your parents like? ....
....
....
....
....
....
....
....

Family

How was your relationship with your parents? ·····································

···

···

···

···

···

···

···

···

···

···

Do you have any siblings? What were they like growing up? ·················

···

···

···

···

···

···

···

Family

Who were your favorite relatives? ....

....

....

....

....

....

....

Do you remember any of the stories your grandparents used to tell you? ....

....

....

....

....

....

....

....

....

....

....

Family

How did you and grandma/grandpa meet? ···

···

···

···

···

···

···

···

Do you remember any songs that you used to sing to your children? ·······················

···

···

···

···

···

···

···

···

···

···

···

Family

Were your grandparents well-behaved? ·······································

··

··

··

··

··

··

What were your parents like? ···

··

··

··

··

What were your grandparents like? ··

··

··

··

··

··

FAMILY HERITAGE

Where are your parents' families from? ....

....

....

....

....

....

....

Have you ever been there? What was that experience like? ....

....

....

....

....

....

....

....

....

....

....

FAMILY HERITAGE

What traditions have been passed down in your family? ·······································

···

···

···

···

···

···

···

···

···

Do you remember any traditional story about your family? ·······························

···

···

···

···

···

···

···

···

FAMILY HERITAGE

What are the classic family stories? Jokes? Songs? ···

··

··

··

··

··

··

··

··

··

Do you remember any traditional story about your family? ·····························

··

··

··

··

··

··

··

··

··

Other Things

....

....

....

....

....

....

....

....

....

....

....

....

....

....

....

....

....

....

....

....

....

Other Things

...career

Chapter 4:
career

As your child, I have always been curious about your professional journey, the highs and lows, the successes and failures, and everything in between. I want to know how you got to where you are today, what inspired you, what challenged you, and what you learned along the way.

But this isn't just about my curiosity. I think there is real value in reflecting on your career path, both for your own personal growth and for our family as a whole. By sharing your story with me, you can help me understand you better as a person and a parent, and inspire me to pursue my own dreams and goals. Moreover, by taking the time to reflect on your own experiences, you may gain new insights and perspectives that could be useful for your future endeavors.

I know that talking about one's career can be difficult, especially if there were hardships or setbacks along the way. But I want you to know that I am here to listen without judgment, and to appreciate and celebrate your achievements as well as your challenges. I want to understand the human behind the professional, the person who persevered through tough times and emerged stronger on the other side.

So, in this chapter, I would like to ask you a series of questions about your career, ranging from the early days to the present. Some of these questions may be easy to answer, while others may require more reflection and soul-searching. But I hope that by going through them, you will gain a deeper appreciation of your own journey, and that we can bond over the shared experience of exploring your life story.

Thank you for taking the time to read this, and for considering sharing your career story with me.

This or That

WEEKEND ACTIVITIES

Read books	Listen to a podcast
Cook food	Order in
Wake up early	Wake up late
Sleep early	Sleep late
Alone time	Family time
Learn a new dish	Learn a new skill
Do chores	Declutter
Workout	Relax
Movie marathon	TV series binge watching

School

Did you enjoy school? ··

··

··

··

··

··

··

What kind of student were you? ···

··

··

··

··

What would you do for fun? ··

··

··

··

··

··

··

School

How would your classmates remember you? ....

....

....

....

....

....

....

Are you still friends with anyone from that time in your life? ....

....

....

....

....

What are your best memories of grade school/high school/college/graduate school? ....

....

....

....

....

....

....

School

Worst memories? ··

··

··

··

··

··

··

··

··

Was there a teacher or teachers who had a particularly strong influence on your life? Tell me about them.
··

··

··

··

··

··

··

··

··

Career

Describe the work that you do. ···

··

··

··

··

··

··

··

··

··

Tell me about how you got into your line of work.·······························

··

··

··

··

··

··

··

··

··

Career

Do you like your job? ···

··

··

··

··

··

··

··

··

What did you think you were going to be when you grew up? ······························

··

··

··

··

··

··

··

Career

What did you want to be when you grew up? ···

···

···

···

···

···

···

···

···

···

What lessons has your work life taught you? ···

···

···

···

···

···

···

···

···

···

Career

If you could do anything now, what would you do? Why?·····················

···

···

···

···

···

···

···

···

···

Do you plan on retiring? If so, when? How do you feel about it? ·············

···

···

···

···

···

···

···

···

Career

Do you have any favorite stories from your work life? ··

··

··

··

··

··

··

··

··

··

··

··

··

··

··

··

··

··

··

Other Things

....

....

....

....

....

....

....

....

....

....

....

....

....

....

....

....

....

Other Things

...love and relationship

Tell it All Books

this or that

Forest	Mountain
America	Europe
Summer	Winter
Pack Light	Overpack
Local food	Fancy reSto
Glamping	Camping
Hotel	Airbnb
Small town	City life

Chapter 5:
love and relationship

I want to take a moment to talk to you about the importance of love and relationships in our lives. As your child, I have always looked up to you as a role model and have learned so much from you. But as I grow older, I am starting to realize that there are things about you that I don't know, and one of those things is your experiences with love and relationships.

I understand that talking about emotions and relationships may not come naturally to everyone, but I want you to know that this is a safe and judgment-free space. Our relationship is built on trust and honesty, and I believe that sharing your experiences with me will only strengthen our bond.

I believe that understanding your experiences with love and relationships will give me valuable insight into the person you are and the values you hold dear. It will also help me understand myself better and give me a greater appreciation for the love that we share as a family.

As you work through this guided journal, I encourage you to be open and honest about your experiences, both the good and the bad. I know that some memories may be painful to revisit, but I believe that the act of writing them down and reflecting on them can be cathartic and healing.

Thank you for taking the time to do this with me. I am grateful for your willingness to share your experiences and for being the wonderful father that you are.

Friendships

Who Was you best friend? ···

··

··

··

··

··

··

··

What was your first memory of your best friend ···

··

··

··

··

··

··

··

··

··

Friendships

What things makes such good friends? ....

....

....

....

....

....

....

....

How would you describe your friends? ....

....

....

....

....

....

....

....

....

....

....

Friendships

How would you describe yourself to your friends?

What is the presents situation of friendships

How frequently do you communicate with your friends?

Love & Relationships

Do you have a love of your life? ··

··

··

··

··

··

··

When did you first fall in love? ···

··

··

··

··

Can you tell me about your first kiss? ···

··

··

··

··

··

Love & Relationships

What was your first serious relationship? ··

··

··

··

··

··

··

··

Do you ever think about previous lovers? ··

··

··

··

··

··

What lessons have you learned from your relationships?·····························

··

··

··

··

··

Love & Relationships

Who were the "ones that got away" in your life? ·······························

··

··

··

··

··

··

··

What was the hardest break up you've ever experienced? ·····················

··

··

··

··

··

Do you remember the best date you ever went on? ····························

··

··

··

··

··

Marriage & Partnership

How did you meet your spouse/partner? ···

···

···

···

···

···

···

···

How did you know they were "the one"? ···

···

···

···

···

How did you propose? ···

···

···

···

···

Marriage & Partnership

What were the best times? ....

....

....

....

....

....

....

....

....

The most difficult times? ....

....

....

....

....

....

....

....

....

Marriage & Partnership

What advice do you have for young couples? ··

··

··

··

··

··

··

··

Do you have any favorite stories from your marriage or about your partner? ··········

··

··

··

··

··

··

··

··

Other Things

Other Things

...parenting

Tell it All Books

this or that

sunrise	sunset
sweet	savory
sun	moon
early bird	night owl
take a risk	just relax
park	beach
family time	me time
bar	cafe
diy	buy
tv series	movies

Tell it All Books

Chapter 6:
parenting

Before you begin, I want to express my gratitude to you for being my father. You have played a significant role in shaping the person that I am today. As I grow older, I realize how important it is to understand your journey as a parent. Your experiences, your struggles, and your triumphs can help me navigate my own journey through life.

This chapter is all about your role as a parent. It's a chance for you to reflect on your experiences as a father and share them with me. I understand that this may be a difficult exercise for you, but I want you to know that it's important to me. Knowing your story will help me understand myself better and deepen our relationship.

As a daughter/son, I want to know about the moments that made you proud, the times you struggled and how you overcame those challenges. I want to know about your parenting style, the values you instilled in me, and how you dealt with difficult situations.

Through this exercise, I hope to gain a deeper appreciation for your journey as a parent. I hope to learn from your experiences and gain insights that I can apply to my own life.

Dad, I know this may not be an easy process for you, but I hope you will consider taking the time to reflect on your journey as a parent. Your story is an important part of who you are, and I am eager to learn from it. I want to thank you in advance for being open and honest with me. I appreciate your willingness to share your story and look forward to learning more about you as a parent.

Parenting

When did you first find out that you'd be a parent? How did you feel? ·····················

....

....

....

....

....

....

....

....

Did you always know you wanted to be a parent? ···

....

....

....

....

....

....

....

....

Parenting

Can you describe the moment when you saw your child for the first time? ·············

··

··

··

··

··

··

··

··

How has being a parent changed you?···

··

··

··

··

··

··

··

··

Parenting

What have you learned about yourself from being a parent? ··

....

....

....

....

....

....

....

What are your dreams for your children? ··

....

....

....

....

....

....

....

....

Parenting

Do you remember when your last child left home for good? ···

···

···

···

···

···

···

···

···

Do you have any favorite stories about your kids?···

···

···

···

···

···

···

···

···

Other Things

Other Things

...health
&
religion

Tell it All Books

Chapter 7:
Health

As a father, you are the cornerstone of your family, providing guidance, support, and love to your children. Your children look up to you as their role model, and they want to know everything about you, including your health history.
This chapter is about your health, and it is important for you to take the time to reflect on your health history and share it with your children. You may not realize it, but your health history can have a significant impact on your children's health and well-being.
Sharing your health history with your children can help them understand their own health risks and take proactive steps to prevent or manage any health issues they may face.

Additionally, knowing your health history can help your children make informed decisions about their own health care and potentially catch any issues early on.
It's important to be honest and open with your children about your health history, even if it includes difficult or embarrassing topics. By sharing your experiences, your children can learn from your successes and mistakes, and they may even feel more comfortable talking to you about their own health concerns.
Remember, your children love and respect you, and they want to know everything about you, including your health history. So take the time to reflect on your health journey and share it with your children. It's a gift that can make a real difference in their lives.

Tell it All Books

this or that

Sport Edition

Aquatic	Golf
Archery	Gymnastics
Badminton	Football
Basketball	Pentathlon
Boxing	Table tennis
Taekwondo	Bicycle
Weightlifting	Volleyball
Long jump	Tennis

Tell it All Books

Religion

What is your religion? ....

....

....

....

Can you tell me about your religious beliefs/spiritual beliefs? ....

....

....

....

....

....

....

....

....

....

....

....

....

....

....

Religion

How did you come to your faith? ....

....

....

....

....

....

....

How has your faith evolved over time? ....

....

....

....

....

....

....

....

....

....

....

Religion

What was the most profound spiritual moment of your life? ··

....

....

....

....

....

....

....

....

....

Do you believe in God? ···

....

....

....

....

....

....

....

Religion

How have you experienced God (or a Higher Power) in your life? ································

....

....

....

....

....

....

....

....

....

Do you believe in the after-life? What do you think it will be like? ·······················

....

....

....

....

....

....

....

Serious Illness

Can you tell me about your illness? ···

··

··

··

··

··

··

··

··

··

Do you think about dying? Are you scared?···

··

··

··

··

··

··

··

Serious Illness

Has this illness changed you? ···

···

···

···

···

···

···

···

···

···

···

What have you learned? ··

···

···

···

···

···

···

···

Other Things

....
....
....
....
....
....
....
....
....
....
....
....
....
....
....
....
....
....

Other Things

...Leisure/ Passion/ travelling

Tell it All Books

this or that

Fashion Edition

Shoe	Shirt
Culottes	Hat
Skirt	Jacket
Jeans	Hoodie
Long Dress	Sweater
pajamas	Blouse
Tunic	Flatshoes
Blouse	Headband

Chapter 8:
Travelling/leisure/passion

This chapter is all about your travels and adventures. Your children want to know about the places you've been, the people you've met, and the experiences that have shaped who you are. This exercise is important not only for your children to understand your life story but also for you to reflect on the moments that have made you who you are today.

Traveling is one of the most enriching experiences one can have. It allows us to explore different cultures, try new foods, and make unforgettable memories. It's a chance to step out of our comfort zones and open our minds to new perspectives. But traveling isn't always glamorous. It can be challenging and even scary at times. Getting lost in a foreign city, dealing with language barriers, or experiencing culture shock can all be part of the adventure.

These moments, while difficult, can be some of the most transformative experiences of our lives.

As a dad, sharing your travel stories with your children is an opportunity to teach them about the world and inspire them to explore it for themselves. It's a chance to show them that life is full of unexpected twists and turns, but that's what makes it so exciting.

So, take some time to reflect on your travels and share your stories with your children. They will appreciate getting to know the person behind the dad they know and love, and you may even learn something new about yourself in the process.

Happy journaling!

Also, on leisure and passion, I want to emphasize the importance of sharing this part of your life with your children. Your hobbies and interests may seem trivial, but they play a significant role in shaping who you are as a person, and your children want to know about it.

Your passions and leisure activities offer a window into your inner world, allowing your children to see you as a whole person beyond your role as their father. By sharing your hobbies and interests with your children, you are giving them a glimpse into the things that bring you joy and fulfillment, helping them to understand what makes you tick and what motivates you. Furthermore, sharing your passions with your children can inspire and motivate them to pursue their own interests, allowing them to see that it's never too late to start doing something you love.

So, take some time to reflect on your hobbies and interests. Think about the activities that bring you joy, the things that you love to do in your free time, and the passions that you have pursued throughout your life. Share these with your children and allow them to see the real you beyond the role of a father.

Remember, this exercise is not just for your children's benefit, but also for yours. By reflecting on your passions and hobbies, you may find new ways to reconnect with them and find more joy and fulfillment in your life.

I encourage you to be open, vulnerable, and honest with your answers to the following questions. Your children will appreciate your candor and will learn more about you in the process.

Favorite Things

What is your favorite color? ···

···

···

···

···

···

···

What is your favorite season? ···

···

···

···

···

···

···

···

···

···

···

···

Favorite Things

What is your favorite car to drive? ··

··

··

··

··

··

··

What is your favorite book? ··

··

··

··

··

··

··

··

··

··

··

Favorite Things

What is your favorite moment in history? ··

··

··

··

··

··

··

What is your favorite perfume/cologne scent? ··

··

··

··

··

··

··

··

··

··

··

··

··

Traveling

What is your favorite country to travel to? ···

···

···

···

···

···

···

···

···

What is your favorite continent to travel to? ···

···

···

···

···

···

···

···

···

Traveling

What is your favorite vacation that you have ever been on?······································

··

··

··

··

··

··

··

What is your favorite picture taken on vacation? ···

··

··

··

··

··

··

··

Traveling

Who is your favorite person to travel with? ···

···

···

···

···

···

···

···

What is your favorite thing to bring with you when traveling?·····································

···

···

···

···

···

···

···

Traveling

What is your favorite food that you have had while on vacation? ·····························

··

··

··

··

··

··

··

··

··

··

··

··

··

··

··

··

··

Other Things

....

....

....

....

....

....

....

....

....

....

....

....

....

....

....

....

....

....

Other Things

....
....
....
....
....
....
....
....
....
....
....
....
....
....
....
....
....
....
....

...note to loved ones

Tell it All Books

Note to Loved Ones

_____

_____

_____

_____

_____

_____

_____

_____

_____

_____

_____

_____

_____

_____

_____

_____

_____

_____

_____

Note to Loved Ones

Tell It All Books

Note to Loved Ones

_____
_____
_____
_____
_____
_____
_____
_____
_____
_____
_____
_____
_____
_____
_____
_____
_____
_____
_____
_____

Note to Loved Ones

_____

_____

_____

_____

_____

_____

_____

_____

_____

_____

_____

_____

_____

_____

_____

_____

_____

_____

_____

_____

_____

Note to Loved Ones

Note to Loved Ones

_____

_____

_____

_____

_____

_____

_____

_____

_____

_____

_____

_____

_____

_____

_____

_____

_____

_____

_____

conclusion

Throughout my life, I've always looked up to you as my guide and inspiration. As I grow older, I realize how much more there is to learn about your journey and the experiences that have shaped you into the incredible person you are today. I know that your story is a treasure trove of wisdom and insight, and I am truly eager to dive into it together with you.

I understand that opening up about your past might not be easy, and some memories may be harder to share than others. However, I want to assure you that my intention is to foster a deeper connection between us and create a cherished keepsake that will be a testament to our bond for years to come.

Please don't hold back, Dad. I am here to listen, learn, and grow through your stories. Your experiences, your struggles, your triumphs, and your passions—all of these are valuable lessons that I can carry with me and pass on to future generations.

As we embark on this guided journal journey together, I hope that we can create a space of trust, love, and understanding. By sharing your story with me, you're not only allowing me to know you better, but you're also giving us the opportunity to grow closer as a family.

Thank you for considering my request, and I look forward to the incredible memories we'll create as we explore your story together. Let this be our keepsake, a tangible reminder of the love and connection that exists between us, now and always.

Notes

Notes

Notes

....
....
....
....
....
....
....
....
....
....
....
....
....
....
....
....
....
....
....
....
....

Notes

Notes

....

....

....

....

....

....

....

....

....

....

....

....

....

....

....

....

....

....

....

....

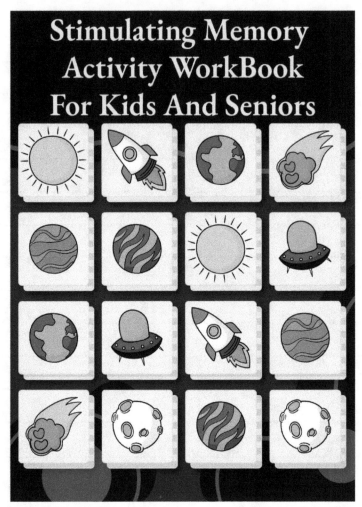

GET THIS BOOK
FREE NOW

Scan This Code
or Visit >>

bit.ly/Einkling

Tell it All Books

Printed in the USA
CPSIA information can be obtained
at www.ICGtesting.com
LVHW081500281023
761972LV00014B/135

9 781961 443150